The Key to Success

By RUSSELL H. CONWELL

FOREWORD

People are thinking, but they can think much more. The housewife is thinking about the chemical changes caused by heat in meats, vegetables, and liquids. The sailor thinks about the gold in sea-water, the soldier thinks of smokeless powder and muffled guns; the puddler meditates on iron squeezers and electric furnaces; the farmer admires Luther Burbank's magical combinations in plant life; the school-girl examines the composition of her pencil and analyses the writing-paper; the teacher studies psychology at first hand; the preacher understands more of the life that now is; the merchant and manufacturer give more attention to the demand. Yes, we are all thinking. But we are still thinking too far away; even the prism through which we see the stars is near the eyes. The dentist is thinking too much about other people's teeth.

This book is sent out to induce people to look at their own eyes, to pick up the gold in their laps, to study anatomy under the tutorship of their own hearts. One could accumulate great wisdom and secure fortunes by studying his own finger-nails. This lesson seems the very easiest to learn, and for that reason is the most difficult.

The lecture, "The Silver Crown," which the author has been giving in various forms for fifty years, is herein printed from a stenographic report of one address on this general subject. It will not be found all together, as a lecture, for this book is an attempt to give further suggestion on the many different ways in which the subject has been treated, just as the lecture has varied in its illustrations from time to time. The lecture was addressed to the ear. This truth, which amplifies the lecture, is addressed to the eye.

I have been greatly assisted, and sometimes superseded, in the preparation of these pages by Prof. James F. Willis, of Philadelphia. Bless him!

My hope is by this means to reach a larger audience even than that which has heard some of the things herein so many times in the last forty-five years. We do not hope to give or sell anything to the reader. He has enough already. But many starve with bread in their mouths. They spit it out and weep for food. Humans are a strange collection. But they can be induced to think much more accurately and far more efficiently. This book is sent out as an aid to closer observation and more efficient living.

RUSSELL H. CONWELL.

September 1917.

RUSSELL H. CONWELL

An autobiography! What an absurd request! If all the conditions were favorable, the story of my public life could not be made interesting. It does not seem possible that any will care to read so plain and uneventful a tale.

I was a young man, not yet of age, when I delivered my first platform lecture. The Civil War of 1861-65 drew on with all its passions, patriotism, horrors, and fears, and I was studying law at Yale University. I had from childhood felt that I was "called to the ministry." The earliest event of memory is the prayer of my father at family prayers in the little old cottage in the Hampshire highlands of the Berkshire Hills, calling on God with a sobbing voice to lead me into some special service for the Saviour. It filled me with awe, dread, and fear, and I recoiled from the thought, until I determined to fight against it with all my power. So I sought for other professions and for decent excuses for being anything but a preacher.

Yet while I was nervous and timid before the class in declamation and dreaded to face any kind of an audience, I felt in my soul a strange impulsion toward public speaking which for years made me miserable. The war and the public meetings for recruiting soldiers furnished an outlet for my suppressed sense of duty, and my first lecture was on the "Lessons of History."

That matchless temperance orator and loving friend, John B. Gough, introduced me to the little audience in Westfield, Massachusetts, in 1862. What a foolish little school-boy speech it must have been! But Mr. Gough's kind words of praise, the bouquets, and the applause, made me feel that somehow the way to public oratory would not be so hard as I had feared.

From that time I acted on Mr. Gough's advice and "sought practice" by accepting almost every invitation I received to speak on any kind of a subject.

While I was gaining practice in the first years of platform work, I had the good fortune to have profitable employment as a soldier, or as a correspondent or lawyer, or as an editor, or as a preacher, which enabled me to pay my own expenses, and it has been seldom in the fifty years that I have ever taken a fee for my personal use. In the last thirty-six years I have dedicated solemnly all the lecture income to benevolent enterprises. If I am antiquated enough for an autobiography, perhaps I may be aged enough to avoid the criticism of being an egotist when I state that some years I delivered one lecture, "Acres of Diamonds," over two hundred times each year, at an average income of about one hundred and fifty dollars for each lecture.

Often have I been asked if I did not, in fifty years of travel in all sorts of conveyances, meet with accidents. It is a marvel to me that no such event ever brought me harm. In a continuous period of over twenty-seven years I delivered about two lectures in every three days, yet I did not miss a single engagement. Sometimes I had to hire a special train, but I reached the town on time, with only a rare exception, and then I was but a few minutes late. Accidents have preceded and followed me on trains and boats, and were sometimes in sight, but I was preserved without injury through all the years. In the Johnstown flood region I saw a bridge go out behind our train. I was once on a derelict steamer on the Atlantic for twenty-six days. At another time a man was killed in the berth of a sleeper I had left half an hour before. Often have I felt the train leave the track, but no one was killed.

Yet this period of lecturing has been, after all, a side issue. The Temple, and its church, in Philadelphia, which, when its membership was less than three thousand members, for so many years contributed through its membership over sixty thousand dollars a year for the uplift of humanity, have made life a continual surprise; while the Samaritan Hospital's amazing growth, and the Garretson Hospital's dispensaries, have been so continually ministering to the sick and poor, and have done such skilful work for the tens of thousands who ask for their help each year, that I have been happy while away lecturing by the feeling that each hour and minute they were faithfully doing good.

Temple University, which was founded only twenty-seven years ago, has already sent out into a higher income and nobler life nearly a hundred thousand young men and women who could not probably have obtained an education in any other institution. The faithful, self-sacrificing faculty, now numbering two hundred and fifty-three professors, have done the real work. For that I can claim but little credit; and I mention the university here only to show that my "fifty years on the lecture platform" has necessarily been a side line of work.

My best-known lecture, "Acres of Diamonds," was a mere accidental address, at first given before a reunion of my old comrades of the Forty-sixth Massachusetts Regiment, which served in the Civil War, and in which I was captain. I had no thought of giving the address again, and even after it began to be called for by lecture committees I did not dream that I should live to deliver it, as I now have done, almost five thousand times. "What is the secret of its popularity?" I could never explain to myself or others. I simply know that I always attempt to enthuse myself on each occasion with the idea that it is a special opportunity to do good, and I interest myself in each community and apply the general principles with local illustrations.

RUSSELL H. CONWELL.

SOUTH WORTHINGTON, MASSACHUSETTS,

September 1, 1913.

OBSERVATION:—EVERY MAN HIS OWN UNIVERSITY

I

OBSERVATION—THE KEY TO SUCCESS

Years ago we went up the Ganges River in India. I was then a traveling correspondent, and we visited Argra, the sacred city of northern India, going thence to the Taj Mahal. Then we hired an ox team to take us across country twenty-two miles to visit the summer home of Ackba, the great Mogul of India. That is a wonderful, but dead city.

I have never been sorry that I traversed that country. What I saw and heard furnished me with a story which I have never seen in print. *Harper's Magazine* recently published an illustrated article upon the city, so that if you secure[Pg 2] the files you may find the account of that wonderful dead city at Futtepore Sicree.

As we were being shown around those buildings the old guide, full of Eastern lore, told us a tradition connected with the ancient history of that place which has served me often as an illustration of the practical ideas I desire to advance. I wrote it down in the "hen tracks" of short-hand which are now difficult to decipher. But I remember well the story.

He said that there was a beautiful palace on that spot before the great Mogul purchased it. That previous palace was the scene of the traditional story. In the palace there was a throne-room, and at the head of that room there was a raised platform, and upon the platform was placed the throne of burnished gold. Beside the throne was a pedestal upon which rested the wonderful Crown of Silver, which the emperor wore when his word was to be actual law. At other times he was no more than an ordinary citizen. But when he assumed that crown, which was made of silver because silver was then worth much more than gold, his command was as absolute as the law of the Medes and Persians.

The guide said that when the old king who had ruled that country for many years died he was[Pg 3] without heirs, leaving no person to claim that throne or to wear that Crown of Silver. The people, believing in the divine right of kings, were unwilling to accept any person to rule who was not born in the royal line. They wasted twelve years in searching for some successor, some relative of the late king. At last the people sank into anarchy, business ceased, famine overspread the land, and the afflicted people called upon the astrologers—their priests—to find a king.

The astrologers, who then worshiped the stars, met in that throne-room and, consulting their curious charts, asked of the stars:

"Where shall we find a successor to our king?"

The stars made to them this reply:

"Look up and down your country, and when you find *a man whom the animals follow, the sun serves, the waters obey, and mankind love*, you need not ask who his ancestors were. This man will be one of the royal line entitled to the throne of gold and the Crown of Silver."

The astrologers dispersed and began to ask of the people:

"Have you seen a man whom the animals follow, the sun serves, the waters obey, and mankind love?"

They were only met with ridicule. At last, in[Pg 4] his travels, one gray old astrologer found his way into the depths of the Himalaya Mountains. He was overtaken by a December storm and sought shelter in a huntsman's cottage on the side of a mountain.

That night, as he lay awake, weeping for his suffering and dying people, he suddenly heard the howl of a wild beast down the valley. He listened as it drew nearer. He detected "the purr of the hyena, the hiss of the tiger, and the howl of the wolf." In a moment or two those wild animals sniffed at the log walls within which the astrologer lay. In his fright he arose to close the window lest they should leap in where the moonlight entered. While he stood by the window he saw the dark outline of his host, the huntsman, descending the ladder from the loft to the floor. The astrologer saw the huntsman approach the door as though he were about to open it and go out. The astrologer leaped forward, and said:

"Don't open that door! There are tigers, panthers, hyenas, and wolves out there."

The huntsman replied:

"Lie down, my friend, in peace. These are acquaintances of mine."

He flung open the door and in walked tiger, panther, hyena, and wolf. Going to the corner[Pg 5] of his hut, the huntsman took down from a cord, stretched across the corner, the dried weeds which he had gathered the fall before because he *had noticed* that those weeds were antidotes for poisoned wild animals. Those poisoned animals had sniffed the antidote from afar and gathered at his door. When he opened that door they followed him to the corner of the hut, in peace with one another because of their common distress. He fed each one the antidote for which it came, and each one licked his hand with thanks and turned harmlessly out the door. Then the huntsman closed the door after the last one, and went to his rest as though nothing remarkable had happened.

This is the fabulous tradition as it was told me.

When the old astrologer lay down on his rug after the animals were gone, he said to himself, "The animals follow him," and then he caught upon the message of the stars and said, "It may be this huntsman is the king," but on second thought he said, "Oh no; he is not a king. How would he look on a throne of gold and wearing a Crown of Silver—that ignorant, horny-handed man of the mountains? He is not the king."

The next morning it was cold and they desired a fire, and the huntsman went outside and gathered some leaves and sticks. He put them in the[Pg 6] center of the hut upon the ground floor. He then drew aside a curtain which hid a crystal set in the roof, which he had placed there because he *had noticed* that the crystal brought the sunlight to a focused point upon the floor. Then the astrologer saw, as that spot of light approached the leaves and sticks with the rising of the sun, the sticks began to crackle. Then the leaves began to curl, little spirals of smoke arose, and a flame flashed forth. As the astrologer looked on that rising flame, he said to himself:

"The sun has lit his fire! The sun serves him; and the animals followed him last night; after all, it may be that he is the king."

But on second thought he said to himself again: "Oh, he is not the king; for how would I look with all my inherited nobility, with all my wealth, cultivation, and education, as an ordinary citizen of a kingdom of which this ignorant fellow was a king? It is far more likely to be me."

A little later the astrologer desired water to drink, and he applied to the huntsman, and the huntsman said, "There is a spring down in the valley where I drink."

So down to the spring went the astrologer. But the wind swept down and roiled the shallow water so that he could not drink, and he went[Pg 7] back and complained of that muddy water. The huntsman said:

"Is that spring rebellious? I will teach it a lesson."

Going to another corner of his hut, he took down a vial of oil which he himself had collected, and, going down to the spring with the vial of oil, he dropped the oil upon the waters. Of course, the surface of the spring became placid beauty. As the astrologer dipped his glittering bowl into the flashing stream and partook of its cooling draught, he felt within him the testimony, "This is the king, for the waters obey him!" But again he hesitated and said, "I hope he is not the king."

The next day they went up into the mountains, and there was a dam holding back, up a valley, a great reservoir of water. The astrologer said, "Why is there a dam here with no mill?" And the huntsman said: "A few years ago I was down on the plains, and the people were dying for want of water. My heart's sympathies went out for the suffering and dying humanity, and when I came back here *I noticed*...."

I may as well stop here in this story and emphasize this phrase. He said, "When I came back here *I noticed*." This is the infallible secret[Pg 8] of success. I wish you to be happy; I wish you to be mighty forces of God and man; I wish you to have fine homes and fine libraries and money invested, and here is the only open road to them. By this road only have men who have won great success traveled.

The huntsman said: "When I came back here *I noticed* a boulder hanging on the side of the mountain. *I noticed* it could be easily dislodged, and *I noticed* that it would form an excellent anchorage in the narrow valley for a dam. *I noticed* that a small dam here would hold back a large body of water in the mountain. I let the boulder fall, filled in for the dam, and gathered the water. Now every hot summer's day I come out and dig away a little more of the dam, and thus keep the water running in the river through the hot season. Then, when the fall comes on, I fill up the dam again and gather the waters for the next year's supply."

When the astrologer heard that he turned to the huntsman and said:

"Do mankind down on the plains know that you are their benefactor?"

"Oh yes," said he; "they found it out. I was down there a little while ago, selling the skins I had taken in the winter, and they came around[Pg 9] me, kissed me, embraced me, and fairly mobbed me with their demonstrations of gratitude. I will never go down on the plains again."

When the astrologer heard that *mankind loved him*, all four conditions were filled. He fell upon his knees, took the horny hand of the huntsman, looked up into his scarred face, and said:

"Thou art a king born in the royal line. The stars did tell us that when we found a man whom the animals followed, the sun served, the waters obeyed, and mankind loved, he would be the heir entitled to the throne, and thou art the man!"

But the huntsman said: "I a king! Oh, I am not a king! My grandfather was a farmer!"

The astrologer said: "Don't talk about your grandfather. That has nothing to do with it. The stars told us thou art the man."

The huntsman replied: "How could I rule a nation, knowing nothing about law? I never studied law!"

Then the astrologer cut short the whole discussion with a theological dictum quoted from the ancient sacred books, which I will give in a very literal translation:

"Let not him whom the stars ordain to rule dare disobey their divine decree."[Pg 10]

Now I will put that into a phrase a little more modern:

"Never refuse a nomination!"

When the huntsman heard that very wise decision he consented to be led down to the Juna Valley and to the beautiful palace. There they clothed him in purple. Then, amid the acclaim of happy and hopeful people, they placed upon his brow that badge of kingly authority—the Silver Crown. For forty years after that, so the old guide said to us, he ruled the nation and brought it to a peace and prosperity such as it had never known before and has never enjoyed since.

That wonderful tradition, so full of illustrative force, has remained with me all the subsequent years. When I look for a man to do any great work, I seek one having these four characteristics. If he has not all four he must have some of them, or else he is good for little in modern civilization.

II

WHO THE REAL LEADERS ARE

Among all of you who read this book I am looking for the kings and queens. I am looking for the successful men and women of the future. No matter how old you may be, you yet have life before you. I am looking for the leading men and women, and I will find them with these four tests. I cannot fail; it is infallible.

Some men, intensely American, will say:

"Oh, we don't have any kings or queens in this country."

Did you ever observe that America is ruled by the least number of people of any nation known on earth? And that same small number will rule it when we add all the women, as we soon shall, to the voting population. America is ruled by a very few kings and queens. The reason why we are ruled by so few is because our people are generally intelligent. "Oh," you will ask, "do you mean the political boss rule?" Yes. That[Pg 12] is not a good word to use, because it is misleading. America is ruled by bosses, anyhow, and it will be so long as we are a free people. We do not approve of certain phases of boss rule, and so don't misunderstand me when I state that a very few persons govern the American people. In my home city, Philadelphia, for instance, nearly two millions of people are ruled by four or five men. It will always be so. Everything depends on whether those four or five men are fitted for the place of leaders or not. If they are wise men and good men, then that is the best kind of government. There is no doubt about it. If all the eighty or ninety millions of people in the United States were compelled to vote on every little thing that was done by the Government, you would be a long time getting around to any reform.

An intelligent farmer would build a house. Will he, as a farmer, go to work and cut out that lumber himself, plane it himself, shape it himself? Will he be the architect of the house, drive all the nails, put on the shingles, and build the chimney himself? If he is an intelligent man he will hire a carpenter, an architect, and a mason who understand their business, and tell them to oversee that work for him. In an intelligent country we[Pg 13] can hire men who understand statesmanship, law, social economics, who love justice. We hire them as skilled people to do what we are not able to do. Why should all the people be all the time meddling with something they don't understand? They employ people who do understand it, and consequently, in a free nation a few specially fitted people will ever be allowed to guide. They will be the people who know better than we know what to do under difficult or important circumstances.

You are ruled by a few people, and I am looking for these few people among my readers. There are some women in this country who now have more influence than any known statesman, and their names are hardly mentioned in the newspapers. I remember once, in the days of Queen Victoria, asking a college class, "Who rules England?" Of course, they said, "Queen Victoria." Did Queen Victoria rule England? During her nominal reign England was the freest land on the face of the earth, and America not half as free if you go to the extremes of comparison. She was only a figurehead, and she would not even express an opinion on the Boer War. It was all left to the statesmen, who had really been selected by the Parliament to rule. They were the real rulers.[Pg 14]

I am looking for the real kings, not the nominal ones, and I shall find the successful men and women of the future by the four tests mentioned in the old tradition of the Silver Crown. The first one is:

"Animals will follow them."

If a dog or cat tags your heels to-morrow remember what I am writing about it here. It is evidence of kingship or queenship. If you don't have a cat or dog or an ox or a horse to love you, then I pity you. I pity the animal the most, but you are also a subject of sympathy. Is there no lower animal that loves to hear your footstep, whines after your heels, or wags the tail or shakes the head at your door? Is there no cat that loves to see you come in when the house has been vacant? Is there no faithful dog that rises and barks with joy when he hears your key in the door? If you have none it is time you had one, because one of the important pathways to great success is along the line of what animal life can give to us of instruction and encouragement.

The time has come when a dog ought to be worth at least a thousand dollars. The time has come when a horse that now trots a mile in 2:05 or 2:06 ought to trot a mile in fifty-five seconds. That is scientifically possible. Now, where are[Pg 15] your deacons and your elders and your class leaders that you haven't a horse in your city that will trot a mile in fifty-five seconds?

"Oh," says some good, pious brother, "I don't pay any attention to trotting-horses! I am too religious to spend time over them."

Is that so? Who made the trotting-horse? Who used the most picturesque language on the face of the earth, in the Book of Job, to describe him? Did you ever own a trotting-horse? Did you ever see a beautiful animal so well fed, so well cared for, trembling on that line with his mane shaking, his eyes flashing, his nostrils distended, and all his being alert for the leap? And did you hear the shot and see him go? If you did and didn't love him, you ought to be turned out of the church.

The time has come when a horse may be as useful as a university.

At Yale University, one day, I heard a professor of science tell those boys that a horse has within its body so much galvanic or electric force continually generated by the activities of life, that if that electricity could be concentrated and held to a certain point, a horse could stand still and run a forty-horse power electric engine. He went further than that and said that a man has within his living body sufficient continually generated[Pg 16] electricity which, if it were brought to a point, might enable him to stand still and run a ten-horsepower electric engine. I went out of that class-room with a sense of triumph, thinking:

"There is going to be use, after all, for the loafers who stand on the corners and smoke!"

In Europe, some years ago, a sewing-machine was invented on which a lady put her bare feet, and her electric forces started the machine. This power does not yet run the machine strong enough to force the needle for real sewing. The only question is to get more of the electricity of that lady through the machine and secure the greater power. Then if a young man wants a valuable wife he must marry one "full of lightning."

The time is very near at hand when all the motive power of the world may be furnished by animal life. When they get one step further the greatest airships will go up and take with them a lap dog. The airship will require no coal, no oil, but just the electric force of that lap dog; and if they carry up enough to feed that dog he will furnish the power to run the motors. The great high seas of the air will be filled with machines run by lap dogs or the electricity of the aviator himself. It is not so far away as many of you[Pg 17] may suppose, and it is the greatly needed improvement of this time, not so much for the purpose of the war, as for peace.

The time has come when an old hen may become a great instructor of the world. I would rather send my child to an old hen than to any professor I ever saw in my life. That old biddy which scratches around your door, or who cackles beside your fence, or picks off your flowers, knows more of some things than any scientific professor on the face of the earth. I wish I knew what that old hen does. But there are some professors who pretend to have a wonderful intellect, who say:

"I graduated from Leipsic or from Oxford or Harvard, and I have no time to observe a hen."

No time to notice a hen? My friend, did you ever try to talk with her?

"No, I did not; she has no language."

Didn't you ever hear her call the chickens and see them come? Didn't you ever hear her scold the rooster, and see him go? Well, a hen does have a real language, and it is time you scientific professors understood what that old biddy says.

"Oh, but," says the professor, "I have no time to spend with a hen! They are around the place all the time, but I never take any special notice[Pg 18] of them. I am studying the greater things in the world."

"Won't you come into my study a minute, professor, and let me examine you? You have examined the boys long enough, now let me examine you.

"Bring all you know of science and all the scientific applications ever made, and all the instruments that are ever used, bring all that the world has ever discovered of chemistry. Come, and take in your hand a dove's egg, just the egg. Now, professor, will you tell the person who is reading this book where, in this egg, is now the beating heart of the future bird? Can you tell where it is?"

"Oh no, I cannot tell that. I can tell you the chemistry of the egg."

"No, I am not looking for that. I am looking for the design in the egg. I am looking for something more divinely mysterious than anything of chemistry. Now, professor, will you tell me where in that egg is the bony frame that next will appear?"

"No, I cannot tell you that."

"Where is the sheening bosom, and where the wings that shall welcome the sun in its coming?"

"No man can tell that," says the professor.[Pg 19]

The professor is quite right. It cannot yet be told. Yet, in that egg is the greatest scientific problem with which the world has ever grappled—the beginning of life and the God-given design. In that egg is the secret of life. Professor, tell me where this life begins. The professor says, "No man can answer questions like that."

Then, until we can answer, we must take off our hats every time we meet a setting hen. For that old biddy knows by instinct more about it than any one of us. She knows directly, through her instinctive nature from God, something about the beginnings of life that we cannot understand yet.

The last time I saw Dr. Oliver Wendell Holmes, the grand poet of Massachusetts, he asked me to go out in his back yard and see his chickens. He told me they would answer to their names. But it turned out that they were like our children, and would not show off before company. But I haven't any doubt those little chickens still with the hen did answer to their individual names when she alone called them. I am sure that great man understood the hen and chickens as fully as Darwin did the doves.

It was a wonderful thing for science that men like Holmes and Darwin could learn so much from[Pg 20] the hen. It reminds me of a current event in Doctor Holmes's own life, though the biographies do not seem to have taken notice of it. He and Mr. Longfellow were very intimate friends. They were ever joking each other like two boys, always at play whenever they met. One day, it is said, Doctor Holmes asked Mr. Longfellow to go down to Bridgewater, in Massachusetts, to a poultry show. He went; he was greatly interested in chickens.

Those two great poets went down to the poultry show, and as they walked up the middle passageway between the exhibits of hens and chickens they came to a large poster on which was a picture of a rooster. He had his wings spread and mouth open, making a speech to a lot of little chickens. It was such a unique picture that Mr. Longfellow called Doctor Holmes's attention to it, and said:

"There, you love chickens, you understand them. What do you suppose a rooster does say when he makes a speech to chickens like that?"

They went on, and Doctor Holmes was studying over it. Finally he turned around and said, "Go on, I will catch up with you." He went back to that poster, got up on a chair, took the tacks out of the top, turned in the advertisement at the[Pg 21] top, above the picture, and then took his pencil and drew a line from the bill of the rooster that was making that speech up to the top. There he wrote what he thought that rooster was saying to those chickens. They say that he did not make a single correction in it, of line or word. He then went after Mr. Longfellow and brought the great poet back to see the poster. He had written these words, in imitation of Longfellow's "Psalm of Life":

Life is real, life is earnest!And
the shell is not its pen;Egg thou
art, and egg remainest,Was not
spoken of the hen,

Art is long, and Time is
fleeting,Be our bills then
sharpened well,And not like
muffled drums be beating,On
the inside of the shell.

In the world's broad field of
battle,In the great barnyard of
life,Be not like those lazy
cattle!Be a rooster in the strife!

Lives of roosters all remind
us,We can make our lives
sublime,And when roasted,
leave behind usHen tracks on
the sands of time.[Pg 22]

Hen tracks that perhaps
anotherChicken drooping in the
rain,Some forlorn and hen-
pecked brother,When he sees,
shall crow again.

Animal life can do much for us if we will but study it, take
notice of it daily in our homes, in the streets, wherever we are.

III

MASTERING NATURAL FORCES

It has been demonstrated by science that the mentality and
disposition of all kinds of animal life are greatly affected by

what they eat. Professor Virchow, of Germany, took two little kittens and fed them on different foods, but kept them in the same environment. After three months he went in and put out his finger at one of those little kittens, and it stuck up its back and spit and scratched and drew the blood. It was savage. He put out his finger to the other kitten, fed on the other food, and it rubbed against his finger and purred with all the loveliness of domestic peace. What was the difference between the kittens? Nothing in the world but what they ate.

Now I can understand why some men swear and some women scratch. It is what they eat.

The universities of the world are now establishing schools of domestic science for the purpose[Pg 24] of training people to understand the chemistry of digestion and the chemistry of cooking. Oh, there is an awful need of better cooks! Yet the fashionable aristocratic American lady thinks it is altogether beneath her dignity to cook a pie or pudding, or boil potatoes. How short sighted that is! The need of better cooks is great. How many a man fails in business because his wife is a poor cook. How many a student is marked down because of the bad biscuit in the boarding-house. Oh yes, and how many a grave in yonder cemetery would be empty still if there had been a good cook in that house.

I have grappled with an awful subject now—the need of better cooks. A man can't even be pious with the dyspepsia. The American lady, so called, who sits in the parlor amid the lace curtains and there plies her needle upon some delicate piece of embroidery, and commits the wonderful chemistry of the kitchen to the care of some girl who doesn't know the difference between a frying-pan and a horse-rake, is not fit to be called an American lady. Any fool could sit amid the curtains, but it takes a giant mind to handle the chemistry of the kitchen. If women forsake that throne of power, men must take it, or our civilization must cease.[Pg 25]

But I will not follow this thought into the thousands of discoveries animals suggest, because, in this wonderful tradition, the real king was not only followed by animals, but "the sun served him, and the waters obeyed him." Now I can combine those two thoughts for illustration, using the wonderful locomotive which draws our railway trains. The locomotive has within it the coal, which is the carbon of the sun. Thus the sun serves man by heating the water; and there is the water changing to steam and driving the piston-rods over the land, obeying man.

We need so much to travel faster than we do now. I saw a man not long ago who said he did not like to travel a mile a minute in a railway train. If you don't go faster than a mile a minute ten years from now you will feel like that old lady who got in a slow train with a little girl. The conductor came through and asked for a ticket for the little girl, and the old lady said:

"She is too young to pay her fare."

"No," said the conductor. "A great girl like that must pay her fare."

"Well," the mother replied, "she was young enough to go for nothing when we got in this train."

You will feel like that if you don't travel faster[Pg 26] than a mile a minute ten years from now. The time is soon coming when, in order to go from Philadelphia to San Francisco, you will get in the end of a pipe or on a wire, and about as quick as you can say "that" you will be in San Francisco. Is that an extravagant expression? The time draws nigh when you won't say that is an extravagant expression. As I am writing this a company to lay that long-contemplated pneumatic tube from New York to Boston is being formed. They have been fighting in the courts over the right to lay it. When they finish it you can put a hundredweight of goods in the New York end of it, and it will possibly land in Boston in one minute and fifty-eight seconds. Now, then, what is to hinder making a little larger pipe and putting a man in and sending him in one minute and fifty-eight seconds? The only reason why you cannot send them with that lightning speed is for the same reason, perhaps, that the Irishman gave when he fell from a tall building and they asked, "Didn't the fall hurt you?" "No, it was not the falling that hurt me, it was the stopping so quick." That is all the difficulty there is in using now those pneumatic tubes for human travel.

We need those inventions now. We are soon[Pg 27] going to find the inventors. Will you find them graduating from some university, or from some great scientific school at Harvard, Yale, Oxford, or Berlin? It may be. I would not say, while presiding over a university myself, that you would not find such people there. Perhaps you will.

But come back in history with me a little way and let us see where these men and women are to be found. Go into northern England, and go down a coal shaft underground two miles, and there is a young man picking away at a vein of coal a foot and a half thick. His hair sticks out through his hat, his face is besmirched, his fingers are covered with soot. Yet he is digging away and whistling. Is he a king? One of the greatest the world has ever seen. Queen Victoria, introducing her son, who has since been king, to that young man, said to him:

"I introduce you, my son, to England's greatest man."

What! This poor miner, who has never been to school but a few months in his life? While he had not been to a day school, he had been learning all the time in the university of experience, in the world's great university—*every-day observation*. When such a man graduates he gets the highest possible degree—D.N.R.—"Don't Need[Pg

Recommends." Let us go in the mine and ask the miner his name.

"Young man, what is your name?"

"Stevenson."

The inventor of the locomotive itself! Oh, where are thy kings, oh, men? They may be in the mine, on the mountain, in the hovel or the palace, wherever a man notices what other people have not seen. Wherever a man observes in his every-day work what other people have not noticed, there will be found the king.

Are any of my readers milkmen? Are you discouraged when the brooks freeze up in the winter? Now, there was a milkman in West Virginia, not many years ago, who went to the train every morning with the milk from the farm, and while they were putting the milk in the car he studied the locomotive standing in the station.

"What do you know about a locomotive?"

"Oh, I don't know anything about it."

Is that so? You have seen and ridden after them all your lifetime, and you have seen them standing in the station, you have looked at the immense structure with some respect, but you don't know anything about it—and then you expect to be a successful man! That young man[Pg 29] became interested in the locomotive, and while he stood around there he watched it, measured it, asked the engineer questions about it. One day the engineer, seeing he was interested, took him down to the switch and showed him how to put on the steam, and how to shut it off, and how to reverse the engine, ring the bell, operate the whistle, and all about it, and he was delighted. He went home and made draftings in the evenings of the locomotive.

Two years after that the same train ran on the siding and the engineer and fireman went into a house to get their breakfast, leaving the locomotive alone—waiting for the snow to be shoveled off the track which had rolled down the mountain. While they were absent a valve of the engine accidentally opened. It started the piston, and the engine began to draw out the train on to the main track, and then it began to go down the fearful grade at full speed. The brakeman went out on the rear platform, caught hold of the wheel brake in order to slow down the train. When he saw the engineer and fireman at the top of the hill swinging their arms as though something awful had happened, the brakeman shouted:

"There is the engineer and fireman, both of them, up there. We will all be killed!"[Pg 30]

The people fainted and screamed, and the cry went to the second car, and then to the baggage car, and that milkman was there. He ran to the side-door to leap, but saw that it would be certain death. Then, with the help of the baggage-man he clambered over the tender, reached the engineer's place, and felt around for the lever in the smoke. When he discovered it he pressed it home. Then reversed the engine. It was a wonder those cylinder heads held. But with an awful crack the driving wheels stopped on the track, shot fire through the snow as they began to roll back against the ongoing train, the momentum still pushing it on. It shook the train until every pane of glass was broken. When it came to a stop the passengers climbed out to ascertain who stopped the train. They discovered that this young man had done it, and saved their lives, and they thanked him with tears.

A stockholder in the railroad company, an old man nearly eighty years of age, was on the train. He went into the stockholders' meeting that night and told the story of his narrow escape on that train. Since then that milkman has been one of the richest railroad owners in the world.

What do you suppose has become of the other milkmen who went at the same time to the same[Pg 31] place and sat on the edge of the platform and swung their feet? What has become of them?

Ask the winds that sweep down from the Alleghany mountains—where are the other milkmen? The winds will answer, "They are going to the pump there still."

It was ever the same. Wherever you look, success in any branch of achievement depends upon this ability to get one's education every day as one goes along from the events that are around us now. The king is found wherever a person notices that which other men do not see.

IV

WHOM MANKIND SHALL LOVE

The great scientific men—and we need more—often are not given the full credit that is due them because they have not "graduated" from somewhere. It seems to me there is a feeling in these later days for creating an aristocracy among the men who have graduated from some rich university. But that does not determine a man's life. It may be a foolish tyranny for a little while, but nevertheless every man and woman must finally take the place where he and she are best fitted to be, and do the things that he and she can do best, and the things about which he and she really know. Where they graduated, or when, will not long count in the race of practical life.

We need great scientific men now more than we ever needed them before. Where are you going to find them? We won't find them where that scientific man came from who invented an[Pg 33] improvement upon the cuckoo clock. His clock, instead of saying, "Cuckoo, cuckoo, cuckoo," when it struck the hour, said, "I love you! I love you! I love you!" That man left the clock at home with his wife nights while he was around at the club, thinking that would be sufficient protestation of his love. Yet any man knows you cannot make love by machinery. That was only a so-called scientific idea.

I read not long ago that a great scientific man said that "love and worship are only the aggregate results of physical causes." That is not true. Love and worship are something beyond physical causes. Educated men ought to know better than to say anything like that.

There are many valuable things that every man knows until he has unlearned them in a university.

There is danger that a man will get so much education that he won't know anything of real value because his useless education has driven the useful out of his mind. It is like a dog I owned when a boy. He was a very good fox dog. One day I thought I would show him off before the boys. We let the fox out at the barn door, which was open just far enough for the dog to see the fox start. Then he began whining and yelping[Pg 34] to get out. I ran out and dropped some red pepper where the dog was likely to follow the fox over the hill. Then I went back and opened the door. The dog rushed out after the fox, but soon began to take in the red pepper. Then he began to whine and yelp—and stopped, whirled around, and, rushing down to the brook, put his nose under the water. From the time he graduated from that pepper university he never would follow a fox at all. He had added education in the wrong direction, and so it is often with these scientific men.

Do you know that the humblest man, whatever his occupation, really knows instinctively certain things better for not having been to school much? It is so easy to bias the mind.

When the boy comes to learn geometry the teacher will say: "Two parallel lines will never run together." The boy may look up and ask, "What is the use of telling me that?" Every man knows that two parallel lines will never run together. But how does he know it? It is born with him. His natural instincts tell that to him. It is what we call "an axiom"—a self-evident truth. It is above argument and beyond all possible reasoning. We know that "two halves are equal to the whole"! You know that[Pg 35] when you cut an apple in half the two halves are equal to the whole of it. You tell that to a geometry class, and they say: "I know that. Everybody knows it." Of course everybody does, because it is a natural scientific fact that you cannot reasonably question.

Ask a man, "Do you know that you exist?" He looks with astonishment and says: "Certainly! Don't I know that I am? I know that I am here, that this is me, that I am not Mrs. Smith or some one else?"

Of course you do. But how do you know it? By a God-given instinct that came into the world with you.

No scientist or school on earth could disprove that, or prove it, either. It is a self-evident fact. I know that I am an intelligent personal identity, and that I dwell in this body in some mysterious way. I know that is my hand, but what I possess is not me. I know by an instinct infallible that I am a spiritual being, separate from this material. You know that. No scientist can prove or disprove it. It is a fact we all know. I know that I can never die, and you know it unless you have gotten educated out of it. It is in your very life; it is a part of your original instinct.[Pg 36]

When some graduate of some great university shall come to you, young man, and say, "I can prove to you that the Bible is not true," or, "I can prove to you that your religion is false," you can say to him: "You are nothing but an educated fool. Because the more you have studied the less truth you seem to know."

It is only one's own personal self that can know his own religious instincts. It is only himself that can know whether he is in spiritual relation to God or not. No education on earth can overturn the fact, although wrong study may confuse the mind.

When a man comes to me, with his higher education, to overturn religion, it reminds me of what Artemus Ward said to that lordly graduate of Oxford and Cambridge. This man told Ward that he was disgusted with his shows. Artemus Ward asked him, "What do you know about these shows?" and he said: "I know everything about them. I graduated from two universities." Then Artemus Ward said, "You remind me of a farmer in Maine who had a calf that stole the milk of two cows, and the more milk he got the greater calf he was." Such is the effect sometimes of education on religious life—the more mental education of some kind which you get the less[Pg 37] you may know about your natural religious instincts.

There is a great need to-day, and prayers go up to heaven now for men and women whom *mankind shall love*—love because they are great benefactors; love because, while they are making money or gaining fame or honor for themselves, they are blessing humanity all the way along. I must not argue now. I will illustrate, because you can remember the illustrations and you might forget an argument.

There is a great need for artists. There never was such a need in the progress of Christian civilization as there is now for great painters. All these walls ought to be covered with magnificent paintings teaching some great divine truth, and every school-house, yes, every barn, ought to have some picture upon it that will instruct and inspire. All our children seek to go to the moving pictures, and that shows what an agency there is in pictures for the instruction of mankind. We need artists by the thousands. It is not a surprise to me that a

New York man is getting a salary of $35,000 a year for moving-picture work because "he notices something other people have not seen." It is no surprise that a great store in that city pays an advertising[Pg 38] man $21,000 a year salary. He can see what the rest of the public does not see.

We need great artists, hundreds of them. Where are you going to find them? You will say "at the art school, in the National Gallery in London, or at the Louvre in Paris, or in Rome." Well, it may be that you will. But it is an unfortunate thing for your theory that one of the greatest painters in America painted with a cat's tail. It is another enlightening thing that the man who received the highest prize at the World's Fair in Chicago for a landscape painting never took "a lesson" in color or drawing in his life.

But that doesn't argue against lessons nor against schools or universities. Don't misunderstand me in this. I am only making emphatic my special subject.

He took the highest prize and never went to an art school in his life. If he had attended school the teacher might have tried to show him something and thus weakened his mind. The teacher in a school who shows a child anything that that child could work out for himself is a curse to that child. It is an awful calamity for a child to be under the control of a too kind-hearted teacher who will show him everything.

One of the greatest artists was Charlotte[Pg 39] Brontë. She was a wonderful little woman, and I like little women. Did you ever read Longfellow's poem on "Little Women"? It always reminds me so much of Charlotte Brontë. One day he showed me the poem, and I asked him why he did not print it in his book, and he replied, "I don't think it is worth while." Since his death they have given it first rank, and I will quote one verse:

As within a little rose we find the richest dyes,As in a little grain of gold much price and value lies,And as from a little balsam much odor doth arise,So in a little woman there's a gleam of paradise.

Charlotte Brontë was one of those wonderful, wiry, beautiful little cultivated combinations of divine femininity which no man can describe. She had a younger brother on her hands, and when a young woman has a younger brother on her hands if she has a beau, she has her hands full. This younger brother was dull of brains, clumsy of finger and unfitted to be an artist. But his sister was determined he should be a painter, and took him to the shore, to the village and the woods, and said, "Notice everything, and notice it closely." Finally, he did secure a second prize. Then his little sister threw her arms about her brother's neck and[Pg 40] kissed him, and thanked him for getting that prize. That is just like a woman! I never could understand a woman. Of all the mysterious things that the Lord ever put together, a woman is the most mysterious. Charlotte Brontë was like an old lady I used to know up in my native town who thanked her husband, with tears, for having brought up a flock of sheep which she herself fed every morning through the winter before he was out of bed.

Finally, Charlotte Brontë's younger brother became dissipated and died, and then her father died, and when we ministers get to be old we might as well die. She was left without means of support. But when she told her friends, they said: "You have a college education, Charlotte. Why don't you write something?" We now find that the first thing she wrote was "Jane Eyre," the wonderful story for which she at last received $38,000. Queen Victoria invited that humble girl to her palace at Windsor because of her marvelous genius.

How came she to write a book like that? Simply because she had noticed so closely, for her brother's sake, that from the nib of her pen flowed those beautiful descriptions as naturally as the water ripples down the mountain-side. That[Pg 41] is always so. No man ever gives himself for others' good in the right spirit without receiving "a hundredfold more in this present time."

I will go one step farther with this thought. We do need great painters, but we don't want more painters like that man who painted the Israelites coming out of Egypt, representing them with muskets on their shoulders with U.S. on the butts.

But more than artists we need great musicians. There is an awful need of music. We have too much noise, but very little real music. Did you ever think how little you have? Do you suppose a true musician is simply a man who roars down to low B and squeals to high C? What an awful need there is of the music which refines the heart, brightens the mind; that brings glory and heaven down to men. I have not the space here to expand upon that thought—the awful need of humanity for real music. But we don't get it. I do not know why it is. I am not able to explain. But perhaps I can hint at what music is.

At Yale I had to earn my own living, and that is why, for these forty-four years, I have been lecturing exclusively to help young men secure their college education. I arose at four o'clock and worked in the New Haven House from four to[Pg 42] eight to get the "come backs" from the breakfast table so that my brother and I could live. Some days, however, I digged potatoes in the afternoon, and taught music in the evening, although the former was my proper occupation. Sometimes my music scholars would invite me in to play something to entertain their company, and I noticed the louder I played the louder they talked. I often said, "What a low standard of musical culture there is in New Haven!" But I learned something after I left college. I learned I was not a musician.

Had I been a musician they would have listened. That is the only test of real music. There is no other.

If you sing and every one whispers, or you play and every one talks, it is because you are not a musician. I dare tell it to you here, when I would not dare say it to you individually if we were alone. There is no person on earth who gets so many lies to the square inch as a person who drums on a piano.

What is music? Music may be wholly a personal matter and be called music. I remember Major Snow, of my native town, who used to listen to the filing of the saw at the sawmill. How that did screech and scratch until it hurt to our toes![Pg 43] We asked the old major why he went down to the mill Saturday, when he could go any other day. He said: "Oh, boys, you do not understand it. When I was young I worked in a sawmill and I come down here to hear them file that saw. It reminds me of the good old days. It is music to me." He was "educated up" to that standard where filing of a saw was music to him, and so men may be educated in all manner of ways in so-called music. But it is not the real music.

What is true music? I went to a beautiful church in New York to exchange with the pastor, and an officer of the church came down the aisle as I walked in and said to me, "Sir, the choir always opens the service." They did; they opened it! I sat down on the pulpit sofa and waited an embarrassingly long time for something to be done up there. The choir roosted on a shelf over my head. The soprano earned $4,000 a year, and I was anxious to hear her. Soon I heard the rustle of silk up there, and one or two little giggles. Then the soprano began. She struck the lowest note her cultivated voice could possibly touch, and then she began to wind, or rather, corkscrew, her way up and up and up, out of sight—and she stayed up there. Then the second bass began and wound his way down, down,

down—down[Pg 44] to the Hades of sound—and he stayed down there.

Now, was that music? Was it worship? Why, if I had stood in that sacred place and positively sworn at the people it would not have been greater sacrilege than that exhibition up on that shelf! Do you think the living God is to be worshiped by a high-flying, pyrotechnic, trapeze performance in acoustics? Neither worship nor music was there. Music does not consist of a high-flying circus trapeze performance in acoustics.

What is music? Music is such a combination of sound as moves the heart to holier emotions, quickens the brain to brighter thoughts, and moves the whole man on to nobler deeds. That is music. Nothing else is music. You can only find out whether you are a musician or not by *taking notice*, while you sing, whether you hold the attention of the people, and whether you influence their memory and their after character.

V

NEED OF ORATORS

We need great orators. The need is something alarming. I am often called to lecture at the Chautauquas and the lyceums, and the committees often urge me to recommend some man or woman who will fill a place on the public platform. They offer marvelous rewards for those who will do that well. There are no men or women alive, not one known in our land to-day, who could be called a great orator. When I began to lecture, fifty-eight years ago, there were Henry Ward Beecher, Wendell Phillips, George William Curtis, Edward Everett, the greatest orator of his day—and John B. Gough. I esteem it a great honor to have been induced by Mr. Gough to go on the lecture platform. They are all gone, and no successors have appeared.

Liberty and oratory have ever gone together, and always will, hence the need of oratory is especially pressing now.[Pg 46]

Why don't we have orators? The editors say "because the newspaper has come in and goes into every home, and a man on Sunday will read a better sermon in his newspaper than ever was delivered, and will save paying the minister and having trouble with the choir." Now, that time will never come. You will never get along without real orators, no matter how many newspapers you may have. I respect the press. I have had something to do with its work in my lifetime. I have worked upon and owned a daily newspaper. But I must say that there is something, after all, in the shake of a living man's finger, something in the flash of his eye, something in the stamp of his foot, but vastly more in his mesmeric power, which no cold type will ever express! You never can fully express the living man in cold lead.

Why don't we have great orators? I don't think the newspapers are in the way. But other people say to me. "It is the injurious effect of the modern school of elocution, which is now called 'the school of oratory.'" It has only been a few years since all these elocutionary schools changed their names to "schools of oratory" and consequently damaged the prospect of our country. The school of elocution may not be a school of oratory at all. It may be a hindrance to oratory;[Pg 47] it depends on what the teaching is. There is a wide difference between elocution and real oratory. Elocution is an art of expression, which every teacher has, and he teaches his own art. But oratory is the great science of successful speech. The man who gets what he pleads for is an orator, no matter how he calls. If you call a dog and he comes, that is oratory. If he runs away, that is elocution!

Why don't we have greater orators? These schools of elocution remind me of an incident which occurred about seventeen years ago. I don't believe I will hurt any one's feelings now by mentioning it. The professor of elocution was sick one day, and the boys came after me. They wanted me to come because the teacher was away, and I resolved to go and entertain that class and let it pass for a recitation. Professors often do that. When I came into the class-room, I said to the boy on the front seat: "What was the last lesson you had in elocution?" One of the boys said:

> "Peter Piper, pickle-picker, picked six pecks of pickled peppers;If Peter Piper, pickle-picker, picked six pecks of pickled peppers,Where are the six pecks of pickled peppers which Peter Piper picked?"[Pg 48]

That is "lip exercise" in elocution. I said to that young man, "I will not teach elocution. But I wish you would come up and deliver that to this class just as you would to an audience." The boy came up and put his toes together, and his hands by his side, for he had not reached the study of gesture. He yelled very rapidly and loudly:

> "Peter Piper, pickle-picker, picked six pecks of pickled peppers;If Peter Piper, piping, picked six pecks of pickled peppers,Where are the pecks of pickled peppers which Peter Piper picked?"

It was elocution, but it was not oratory. I had trouble in getting up another boy, but I finally did. He thought that oratory consisted entirely in elocutionary "inflections," so he delivered it:

"Peter Piper picked six pecks of pickled peppers;If Peter piping picked a peck of pickled peppers,Where's the peck of pickled peppers Peter Piper picked?"

(With marked raising and lowering of the voice.)

It sounded like an old rooster in the barn in the morning. But being elocution, it was not oratory.[Pg 49]

But the most illustrative and most absurd speech I ever heard was by a visitor in that class that day. He was sitting over near the aisle, and one of the students came and whispered to me: "That young man has graduated from an Eastern school of elocution, and he is going to act the heavy parts in tragedy upon the stage. He is a great elocutionist, and won't you get him to recite something to the class?" I fell into the trap, and went down to the young man, and said: "I understand you are an elocutionist. Will you come up and recite something for the class?"

As soon as he looked up at me I saw by his eyes there was something the matter with his head. I do not know just what, but things have happened since that make it no unkindness to refer to him the way I do. I said: "Please come up and recite something," and he replied: "Shall I recite the same thing the young men have been reciting?" I said, "You don't need to do that; take anything." He left his gold-headed cane—the best part of him—on the floor, and then he came up to the platform and leaned on the table and said to me: "Shall I recite the same thing the young men have been reciting?" I said: "You can if you wish. You are perfectly free to take anything you choose. The professor is away,[Pg 50] anyhow. When the cat is away the mice will play."

Then he began to prepare himself for that recitation. I never saw such behavior in my life. He pulled up his sleeves, brushed back his hair, shook himself, moved the table away forward, and I slid far back by the door and left the platform open, for I didn't know what he was going to do next. Then he gave the selection:

> "Peter Piper picked a peck of pickled pepper-r-rs;If Peter Piper, piping piper, picked a peck of pickled pepper-r-r-rs,Where's the peck of pickled pepper-r-r-rs Peter Piper pickle-picker-r-r picked?"

He rolled in a flutter the letter "r" in each line. That class looked up with awe, and applauded until he repeated it. It was still elocution, but it was not oratory. He thought that oratory consisted of rolling the "r's" and rolling himself. That is not oratory.

Where do they learn oratory? They learn it in the old-fashioned school-house, from that old hen at the kitchen door, in some back office, in some hall, or some church where young men or women get together and debate, saying naturally the things they mean, and then *take notice* of the[Pg 51] effects of what they debate upon, the conviction or after action of those who listen. That is the place to observe. You must *take notice* if you are to be a great orator.

The greatest orator of the future will be a woman. It has not been two months since the management of a women's Chautauqua said, "We could give $40,000 a year to any woman who will be a natural woman on the platform." They would make money at $40,000 a year if they hired a woman who would be a real woman. The trouble is that when women get on the platform they try to sing bass or try to speak as a man speaks. And there is such a need for women orators now! I get provoked about it when I think. Why isn't there a great woman orator like Mrs. Livermore now when she is needed so much?

VI

WOMAN'S INFLUENCE

If women vote they will be of little account unless they are leaders. It is of no special advantage to the voter to ignorantly put a piece of paper in a box. But it is of great account to influence ten thousand votes. That is what women must do if they are going to exercise their right under suffrage—they must be the influence behind the throne, not merely a voter.

When I was a boy in the district school a substitute teacher came in, and we all loved that little woman. We would do anything she asked us to do. One day that substitute teacher, who could not get a first-class certificate, copied a verse of a poem and asked me to read it:

> If you cannot on the oceanSail among the swiftest fleet:Rocking on the mighty billows,Laughing at the storms you meet.[Pg 53]

She asked me to read it once, and then she turned the paper over and said, "Now, Russell, repeat it." I said, "I have not learned it by heart." Said she: "Don't learn it by heart. I will try again." So she wrote the second verse:

> If you are too weak to journeyUp the mountain steep and high.

Then she said to me, "Now, Russell, read it through once, and notice carefully each word, and don't look back at a word a second time." I know not now why she demanded that; I have looked in many books of psychology and in many places to find out. I have no explanation of this, and I ask you to think for me, for this is the fact. I took the second verse and read it through as she told me to do. Then she turned it over and said, "Please repeat it." I said, "I cannot repeat it; I have not learned it by heart." She replied: "Don't you say that again. Just shut your eyes and make a mental effort to see those verses, and then read it."

I shut my eyes and said, "Oh, it is all dark." Then she seemed very much disturbed and said: "Now, Russell, don't say that. Won't you try to do what I ask you to do?"

I thought the little woman was going to cry,[Pg 54] so I said, "Yes, I will do the best I can." She said, "Shut your eyes again and make a determined effort, with your eyes shut, to see that poetry just as though it were right before you." I shut my eyes and made that effort, and saw it as distinctly as though I had held it before my open eyes. So long as my eyes were shut I could see the two verses, and I read it all through, word for word, and I read it backward, word for word, to the beginning.

I thought I had seen a ghost. I went home and told my father what had happened, and he rushed down from the pasture to the school-house and said to the teacher:

"If you indulge again in your foolish superstitions you will never teach in that school-house again."

It must have been uncomfortable for her, and her secret went down to the grave with her, as far as I know. Yet what would I not give if I could place before the world now what that little girl knew. All our educational institutions, for which I have labored all these years, would be as nothing compared with that one secret if I could give it to you—that secret of being able to look upon a scene and shut's one's eyes and bring it all back again, study it in detail.[Pg 55]

I have not had great personal power in that line. But I have seen a man who would take a column of the morning paper and read it down, and hand me the paper and read it through with his eyes shut and scarcely make a mistake. I do not know that I ever saw any one who was infallible, but rarely would he make a mistake. Often he could tell me where the comma, semi-colon, and other marks of punctuation were.

I do not believe there is a normal child who is not mentally capable of that power when he has a teacher who understands how to develop it. That little teacher, who held only a second-class certificate, knew more about psyhology than many of the greatest men who preside over great institutions.

In the Alps some years ago was Professor Slayton, a native of Brighton, England. He was one of the nation's best botanists. His wife died and he was left with a little child between five and six years of age. They boarded at the Hotel Des Alps, in the Chamouni Valley. One morning he took his little girl up to the Mer-de-Glace, and then he told her to run back to the hotel, saying he would return to her in the evening.

She bid her father good-by and saw him go up Mont Blanc into the forest, and she ran back.[Pg 56] He did not return in the evening, and she sat up all night and worried, and early in the morning she ran out from the hotel and ran up the stream to the path she had seen her father take. Then, running across, she started climbing up the side of the great snow-capped mountain. She came suddenly to a place where the path ran around along a projecting precipice, two hundred and eighty feet in the perpendicular, around a promontory of rock that set a few feet back. When she came to that spot her feet slipped upon the snow on the glare ice, and she slid down and down over the edge so far that her fingers just caught in the moss on the edge and one foot rested on about an inch projection of the rock.

As she hung there she screamed, "Papa!" Her father heard that cry. He was down in the valley so far that he could not see her, but he could hear her voice. He recognized it, and he felt there was an awful need of him—"humanity called to him." He ran across the valley and up the path. On the way there was a tree near which he had previously *noticed* there was an ax. He pulled out the ax and ran on to a tree where he had previously *observed* there was a rope which the coal-burners had long used to let coal down from the cliff. He clipped the rope with the ax,[Pg 57] threw away the ax, and, tying the rope around him as he had *noticed* the guides do who take travelers over the "sea of ice," he ran on, until suddenly he came to the spot where his little girl had slipped. He could see the parting in her hair twenty feet down, and all was glare ice between. His heart must have stopped beating. But he suddenly shouted:

"Papa's come. Hold on tight!"

She screamed, "I cannot hold on any longer!"

He turned and threatened her. Oh, ye parents, whosoever you may be, you may save your own son or daughter from a physical or moral death by training them to obey when they are young. Her fingers tightened again, and he threw the rope around the butt of a tree he had *noticed*, and let himself rapidly down over that ice. He tried to get hold of his little child's hands, but they had melted deep into the moss, and he let himself down beside her and caught hold of her dress and pulled her to him.

Both were hanging from the edge of the cliff, and the end of the rope was in his hand, and his hand on the ice. He tried to pull himself up, but the rope would not give an inch, and then he tried to push his little girl up, but with frozen fingers she could not climb.[Pg 58]

There they hung in the high Alps, alone! Will he fall on the jagged rocks and be crushed to death? No, he will not fall, because he is a king. He has used his *every-day observation*, though he is a graduate of a university. He had *noticed* something more—he had observed how the dogs howl when they find perishing travelers. Those St. Bernard dogs, whenever they find a dead body or a man laying insensible, will always howl in one peculiar way. Those dogs know more about acoustics than an architect. How do they know? God told them. When a dog utters that cry it can be heard for miles and miles. The professor imitated the call of the dog, and when it rang down the valley the coal-burners heard it and the wood-choppers heard it. They said:

"That is a dog, and a dog never howls like that unless he has found a dying man." So, throwing down their axes and guns, and running over the snows toward the sound of the call, they suddenly came to the spot. They caught hold of the rope and one of them slid down rapidly and seized the little girl's arm and passed her up, and then caught hold of the professor's arm and lifted him, while the others pulled upon the rope. Thus they dragged him up. The professor fell on the snow-drift and fainted dead away.[Pg 59]

But he was a king. He heard humanity's cry, and when he heard it he knew where the ax was. He had used his every-day study in such a way that he knew where the old rope was, and knew how to tie it, and he knew how to call for help. Whenever you find on earth a successful man or woman you will always find it is a man or woman who hears humanity's call, and who has so used his every-day means of observation that he knows where the weapons are with which to fight those battles, or where the means are with which to bring men relief.

I could not better put into your minds that professor's feelings than by a quotation of an English phrase which he printed in English on his scientific books, though the books were published in French:

> We live for those who love us,For those who know us true;For the heavens that bend above us,For the good that we can do.For the wrongs that lack resistance,For each cause that needs assistance,For the future in the distance,For the good that we can do.

Russell Herman Conwell (February 15, 1843 – December 6, 1925) was an American Baptist minister, orator, philanthropist, author, lawyer, and writer. He is best remembered as the founder and first president of Temple University in Philadelphia, as the Pastor of The Baptist Temple, and for his inspirational lecture, "Acres of Diamonds". He was born in South Worthington, Massachusetts.

The son of Massachusetts farmers, Conwell left home to attend the Wilbraham Wesleyan Academy and later Yale University. In 1862, before graduating from Yale, he enlisted in the Union Army during the American Civil War. Conwell desired to enlist in the war effort shortly after its outbreak in 1861, but could not initially gain the approval of his father, Martin Conwell. His abolitionist father ultimately changed his mind, allowing Conwell to enlist in Company "F" of the 27th Massachusetts Volunteers, better known as the "Mountain Boys". Conwell and the Mountain Boys served in North Carolina and first engaged the opposition at Kinston, North Carolina. There Conwell gained a reputation for self-sacrifice.

During the "Gum Swamp" expedition, he returned to the battlefield to retrieve the bodies of two of his deceased soldiers, and later during the same campaign purposefully drew enemy fire upon his position – resulting in his being shot in the shoulder – in order to gain a tactical advantage on his Confederate adversaries. On September 25, 1862 he was commissioned as a captain (to rank from September 9, 1862) and placed in command of Company F of the 46th Massachusetts Infantry Regiment. He was mustered out of service, along with his regiment, on July 29, 1863.

After his nine-month enlistment, Conwell returned home to Massachusetts to convalesce after contracting a dangerous fever that plagued him throughout the summer of 1863. Upon regaining health, he volunteered for a three-year enlistment in the Second Massachusetts Artillery and was commissioned as a captain in command of Company D on September 9, 1863. He then returned to North Carolina and was placed in command of a fort in Newport Barracks. After his soldiers there had not been paid for three months, Conwell requested and received permission to travel to Newberne to secure remuneration for his men. While he gained permission to cross enemy lines, he did not secure a permit to be absent from this post, nor did it appear that the 21-year-old Conwell understood the distinction. Twenty miles into his trip, Conwell learned that Confederate forces attacked and overran his company's position. When subsequently reported that the absence of Union officers contributed to the loss, Conwell was placed under arrest and detained in Newberne pending an investigation. It is for this incident Conwell has been accused of desertion by his detractors. Conwell was mustered out of the 2nd Massachusetts Heavy Artillery on May 20, 1864. While he claimed that he was later reinstated by General James B. McPherson, no military records confirm his statement.

Two months into his detention, and prior to the completion of the investigation, Conwell was assigned to Nashville, Tennessee, in June 1864 to join General MacPherson's movement against Atlanta. During the battle of Kennesaw Mountain, now Lieutenant-Colonel Conwell's arm and shoulder were broken during battle from an exploding artillery shell. While recovering from this injury, the atheist Conwell converted to Christianity in large part due to the heroism exhibited by his loyal private assistant, John H. Ring.

Upon recovering from this latest injury, Colonel Conwell was assigned to Washington with a dispatch to General Logan. But Conwell's health compelled him to resign and retire from service, whereupon he received an honorable discharge, as well as a certificate for faithful and patriotic service from the Commonwealth of Massachusetts.

After the Civil War, Conwell studied law at the Albany Law School. Over the next several years, he worked as an attorney, journalist, and lecturer first in Minneapolis, then in Boston. Additionally, during this period, he published about 10 books, including campaign biographies of Ulysses S. Grant, Rutherford B. Hayes, and James A. Garfield.

Alexander Reed, a leader of the Grace Baptist Church of Philadelphia, heard Conwell preach when he visited him in Lexington, Massachusetts, and recommended that Conwell become a pastor for his congregation. The official "call" was made on October 16, 1882. Conwell's first sermon at Grace Baptist was on November 30, 1882. At this time the church was located at Berks and Mervine. That building was demolished in 1969 to make way for Temple University's Gladfelter and Anderson Halls

The December 4, 1882 issue of *The Public Ledger* reported the following about the new minister and church:

Dedication of a New Baptist Church services conducted by the Rev. Russell H. Conwell, late of Massachusetts. The church proper on the upper story is in the form of an amphitheatre, and has seating capacity for between six and seven hundred persons. It is finished with great taste and completeness. The ceiling is frescoed, the windows are of stained glass and the pews of hardwood and handsomely upholstered. The edifice cost about $70,000.

Conwell ended evening services by holding an hour of prayer, leading song services, and giving commentary relevant to his sermons. The musical pastor often performed a solo piece during evening services.

Conwell's magnetic personality, high descriptive, practical, and engaging sermons soon drew crowds so large that the church outgrew its capacity to seat all that wanted to come. Reverend Conwell used the story of Hattie May Wiatt and her 57 cents to spur phenomenal fundraising to build a new church. Hattie May lived nearby, and she and other children were gathered outside when Conwell walked up one Sunday morning. Conwell carried Hattie May on his shoulders and sat her in a corner in the back. When he ran into her walking the streets one day, he told her not to worry that one day they'd build a new church so all the children could come in. Hattie May died at six years of age. When she died from diphtheria, she had saved 57 cents to contribute to the cause. The girl's mother told Reverend Conwell that Hattie May had been saving money to help build a bigger church and gave him the coins. Reverend Conwell had the 57 cents turned into 57 pennies, told the congregation the story of little Hattie May, and auctioned the pennies for a return of about $250. In addition, 54 of the 57 pennies were returned to Reverend Conwell, and he later put them up on display.

On June 28, 1886, a nearby house at the corner of Broad and Berks streets, referred to as The Temple because the property owner did not want the house to be called a church until the mortgage was fully paid, was investigated for purchase by the Wiatt Mite Society, which was organized for the purpose of taking the 57 cents and enlarging on them sufficiently to buy the property for the Primary Department of the Sunday school.

A few days later, the congregation agreed to purchase the lot. The first payment for the lot was 57 cents. The property was conveyed to the church on January 31, 1887. In that same house, the first classes of Temple College, later Temple University, were held. The house was later sold to allow Temple College to move and the Baptist Temple (now the Temple Performing Arts Center) to grow, and still, more of that money went towards founding the Samaritan Hospital. This story so touched Conwell that he repeated it many times. The transcript for the sermon where Conwell tells this story in full is available at Temple University Libraries.

In September 1887, at the Centennial Celebration of the United States Constitution, money received from the Wiatt Mite Society was given "for the success of the new Temple". This was the first time the name "Temple" was used in place of the church name.

In 1888, the youth group considered becoming a worldwide organization. The pastor was a speaker at a Christian Endeavor convention. Conwell was very impressed by the purpose and enthusiasm of the group. He later recommended the Christian Endeavor to the youth group of the church. On September 10, 1888, the Society of Christian Endeavor was finally organized. The Christian Endeavor youth groups continued to meet at the Church until the 1960s.

Charles M. Davis, a young deacon, approached the pastor with his desire to preach; however, Davis had little education and was without sufficient funds to continue his studies. Conwell agreed to tutor him. Over the next few days, seven prospective students met with Conwell, and Temple College was conceived. Ultimately, Conwell became Dr. Conwell, president of the college, now known as Temple University.

As the membership continued to grow to over one thousand and the Sunday School to even greater numbers, a larger facility was needed. Consequently, on March 29, 1889, a contract was negotiated to build the new church. The ground was broken for the new building on March 27, 1889, and the cornerstone was laid on July 13, 1889.

On February 15, 1891, Conwell preached his last sermon in the old church at Marvine and Berks Streets. He preached the first sermon at the new building on March 1. Sixty people were baptized in the afternoon, and several addresses were given. The Rev. L. B. Hartman, the first minister, was present. The celebration continued throughout the week, and the church was filled to capacity for all of its services. The new church later became known as The Baptist Temple.

Conwell's name lives on in the present-day Gordon-Conwell Theological Seminary, in South Hamilton, Massachusetts, an interdenominational evangelical theological seminary formed in 1969 by the merging of two former divinity schools, Conwell School of Theology of Temple University in Philadelphia and Gordon Divinity School in Wenham, Massachusetts.

Russell Conwell Middle Magnet School in Philadelphia bears his name as well. The school yearbook is entitled *Acres of Diamonds*. Temple University's football team wear diamond decals on their helmets and diamond trim on their collars to reference Conwell's "Acres of Diamonds" speech.

The film *Johnny Ring and the Captain's Sword* (1921) is based upon Conwell's writings regarding his experiences in the Civil War.

The elementary school in Worthington, Massachusetts, his home town, bears his name

The congregation of the church continues today as the Grace Baptist Church.